A+ books

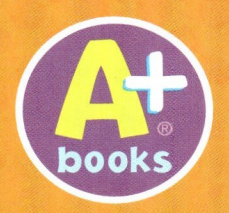

We All Do Something Well

by Shelley Rotner and Sheila Kelly, EdD
photographs by Shelley Rotner

CAPSTONE PRESS
a capstone imprint

Do you know someone who does something well?

3

"I know a girl who can paint very well

and a boy who can climb very high."

"I like to **swim** and learned how to float,

but my little brother is better on **skis.**"

8

We're **happy** when we do **something** well,

whatever that might be.

"Reading is easy for me,

but I'd like to be better at math."

"I can't read very well yet.
I wish I could."

It can take a long time to
be good at something.

Mia knows how to spell.

Sophie prints well.

And Josh is really good with computers.

"I haven't **discovered** what I'm good at yet."

Ethan writes stories.

Beth likes to build.

Olivia made the soccer team.

Gabe sees lots of things in the park.

We all like to **do** what we do **best.**

And when things are hard,
we need help to learn.

"I don't get it."

We're good at different things.

"I feed the baby myself now."

"I can fix my brother's wagon."

"I got my training wheels off early."

"The kids made me captain of our team."

Schoolwork, singing, dancing, playing music or sports!

20

We **all** have something we do **well**.

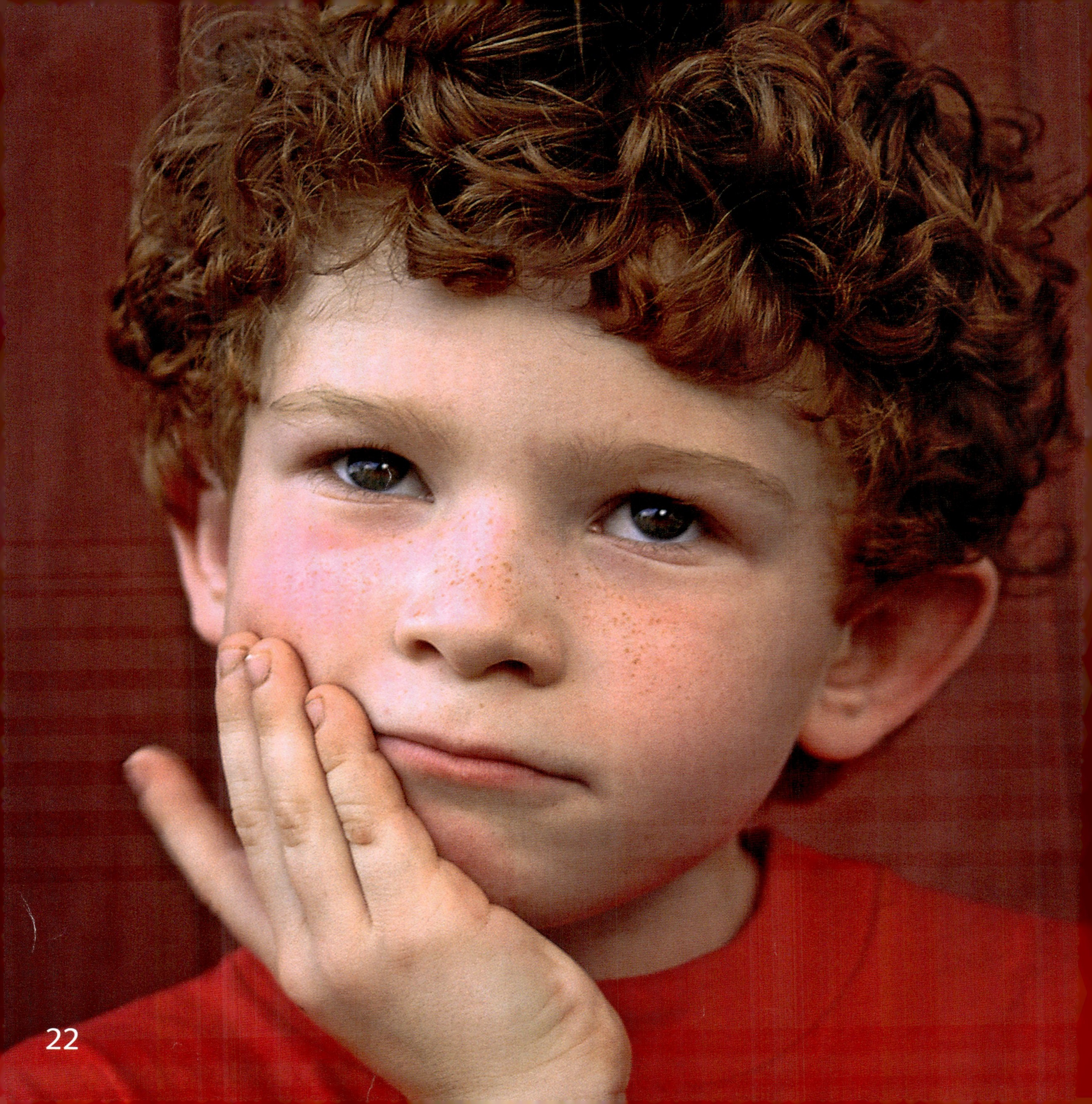

What can **you** do well?

A+ Books are published by Capstone Press,
1710 Roe Crest Drive, North Mankato, Minnesota 56003.
www.capstonepub.com

Text copyright © 2013 by Shelley Rotner and Sheila Kelly. Photographs copyright © 2013 by Shelley Rotner.
All rights reserved. No part of this publication may be reproduced in whole or in part, or stored in a retrieval system, or transmitted in any form or by any means, electronic, mechanical, photocopying, recording, or otherwise, without written permission of the publisher.

Library of Congress Cataloging-in-Publication Data
Rotner, Shelley.
 We all do something well / by Shelley Rotner and Sheila M. Kelly.
   p. cm. — (A+ books. Shelley Rotner's world.)
 Summary: "Full-color photographs and simple text illustrate a variety of skills and abilities people have"—Provided by publisher.
 ISBN 978-1-62065-067-7 (library binding)
 ISBN 978-1-62065-754-6 (paperback)
 ISBN 978-1-4765-1348-5 (ebook PDF)
1. Self-confidence—Juvenile literature. I. Kelly, Sheila M. II. Title.
BF575.S39R68 2013
 153.7'52—dc23   2012033988

Editorial Credits
Jill Kalz, editor; Heidi Thompson, designer; Wanda Winch, media researcher; Jennifer Walker, production specialist

Internet Sites

FactHound offers a safe, fun way to find Internet sites related to this book. All of the sites on FactHound have been researched by our staff.

Here's all you do:

Visit *www.facthound.com*

Type in this code: 9781620650677

Look for all the books in the series:

Different Kinds of Good-byes

Feeling Thankful

We All Do Something Well

What's Love?

Check out projects, games and lots more at
www.capstonekids.com

Printed in the United States of America in North Mankato, Minnesota.
092012   006933CGS13